VINEGAR HILL

ALSO BY COLM TÓIBÍN

VINEGAR HILL

COLM TÓIBÍN

BEACON PRESS, BOSTON

Beacon Press
Boston, Massachusetts
www.beacon.org
Beacon Press books
are published under the auspices of
the Unitarian Universalist Association of Congregations.

Published by arrangement with Carcanet Press.

Printed in the United States of America

25 24 23 22   8 7 6 5 4 3 2 1

This book is printed on acid-free paper that meets the uncoated paper
ANSI/NISO specifications for permanence as revised in 1992.

Text design by Andrew Latimer

Library of Congress Cataloging-in-Publication Data
Name: Tóibín, Colm, 1955– author.
Title: Vinegar Hill / Colm Tóibín.
Description: Boston : Beacon Press, [2022] | Summary: "A wide variety of
    poems, ranging in setting and topic, Vinegar Hill deals with gay
    experience and with the experience of loss, with memory and a fading
    past as well as the present moment"—Provided by publisher.
Identifiers: LCCN 2021054425 | ISBN 9780807006535 (hardcover) |
    ISBN 9780807006542 (ebook)
Subjects: LCGFT: Poetry.
Classification: LCC PR6070.O455 V56 2022 | DDC 821/.914—dc23
LC record available at https://lccn.loc.gov/2021054425

for James Shapiro

CONTENTS

VINEGAR HILL

SEPTEMBER

The first September of the pandemic,
The sky's a watercolour, white and grey,
And Pembroke Street is empty, and so is
Leeson Street. This is the time after time,
What the world will look like when the world
Is over, when people have been ushered into
Seats reserved for them in the luminous
Heavens.
   Moving towards the corner of
Upper Pembroke Street and Leeson Street,
An elderly man wears a mask; his walk is
Sprightly, his movements brisk. I catch
His watery eye for a watery moment.
Without stopping, all matter-of-fact,
He says: 'Someone told me you were dead.'

IN LOS ANGELES

Who can say what he had in mind,
Or where he was headed,
The last man ever to walk a dog?

Water was scarce, and the sun
Burnished the paintings in the
Getty. About suffering, of course,

They were never wrong.
But none of us imagined that
Between two trucks on the 110,

I would see Icarus crawl. His
Bronzed smile and tanned legs
I lover in the mind as much else fades.

I told him about the forgiveness
Of sins, the resurrection of souls,
And life everlasting. But it was,

He said, too little too late.
Lux Aeterna; Tantum Ergo; Dies Irae.
Even the dear old hymns would not

Give light its shade, shade its dark.
People moved through their houses
Wondering where, in the name of God,

They had left their phones, their
Glasses, their e-cigarettes,
Their take on what must now unfold.

CURVES

Within the body is its own sweet sound,
It starts as echo and fades fast.
In the bricked-up burden of bone
Two old notes repeat, both fierce.

The city curves. The brightest will
Is open. I have been here for years.
There are lights and wires; there is
Some beauty. It is almost enough.

MYSTERIUM LUNAE

Last night
I saw that the moon
Was empty in the sky.

The stars around did
What they do.
They are

Millions of miles
Away
Or millions of years,

And are totally exhausted.
But the moon is blank,
Just a space to show

Where it might have
Been. We will tell
Whoever will attend

That the moon used to catch
Light from the sun
And waxed and waned:

Full, sickle, half-
Moon. And the songs:
Blue Moon, Song to the Moon

(From 'Rusalka'),
Moon River, The Dark
Side of the Moon,

The Moon and the Melodies.
It was all the rage, once,
The moon.

It was a large step,
A sad step,
For mankind.

Soon, the sun will run
Out of hydrogen
And it will all

Be gone.
The disappearance
Of the moon

Is just the start.
I am working day and night
On my book,

Knowing it will
Be the final word
On the matter.

I will compose,
With aid from scientists,
A description in concise

Prose, of the time before the bang,
The gorgeous vacancy
The pre-astral soup,

Gravity dancing like
A herring
On the griddle-oh,

And the sly almostness
Of atoms and particles,
And how long a neutron

Took to be certain
That it was not a proton,
And the war

Between infinity and
Eternity that would have
Gone on for ever

Had the world,
Oozing immanence,
Not begun to roll,

With its built-in
Obsolescence,
Its sell-by date,

Its oomph, its ooh-la-la,
Its everything that
Is the case.

It is calm here
Now. Waves have
Stopped, of course.

The sea has settled
Down; soon it will
Be a fly-over state.

There is
Nothing to compel
Its tides.

At gatherings, they read
Matthew Arnold's poem
And marvel

At the lines about the
Sea being calm tonight.
What else is there?

But it wasn't always calm.
I can swear to that.
I remember

Redondo Beach
And the waves high
And the sun

Going down
Over the horizon.
Strange, I have

No memory of the moon.
But it must have been there
Somewhere.

But, no matter what, you can
Look all you want,
The moon is in the past,

Like analogue,
Or the western seaboard,
Or the library at Alexandria,

Or *Sic transit gloria
Mundi,* a lovely
Old saying

Long eclipsed
By more fashionable
Tongues that yet are

Speechless at
The vacancy
In the night sky.

They are
Howling at the
Thing not there

That we want back
Now, or at least
Soon.

THE LONG TRICK

Ingmar Bergman was still alive the time
I sailed on the *Estonia* past the inhabited
Islands beyond Stockholm on a winter Sunday
Just as the dark was descending. I dreamed
That he might come and mournfully wave at us,
Or, that I might be lucky enough to catch
A glimpse of him brooding at twilight,
Knowing how doomed we are, all of us.

This was the same *Estonia* that sank between
Stockholm and Tallinn the following year.
Eight hundred and fifty-two people drowned.
But tonight feels long rather than dangerous.
The man sharing my cabin goes to bed early.
There is a restaurant for Swedes, as there
Always will be, and another, lesser one,
For Estonians, with grim frankfurters

And runny coleslaw. I wish I could recount
Some premonition: that I foresaw the water
Rushing through the narrow corridors, waking
Us up from our sleep, and then everything dark
And people calling out in Baltic languages
And then water covering everything, eventually
Even the ship. But it was ordinary on my night,
And we arrived in Tallinn just as morning did.

It was like that too when I went out on a boat
To the Great Barrier Reef a month or so after
Two divers had been left behind by mistake.
It was simple: with everyone on deck,
The man in charge had shouted: 'Is everyone here?'
And what could the passengers do? They shouted yes!
The two who were missing were skilled
At using oxygen sparingly. So, they were still

Down there, investigating the deep, as the boat
Started its engine and chugged back to Port Douglas.
How clear it must have been once they surfaced
That they would be unlikely to make it back to shore!
I suppose they must have shouted. Maybe they swam
For a while and hoped that the boat would return
For them when their absence was discovered.
They must have really struggled before they died.

On my trip, I was too scared to dive, not because
Of them, the two who disappeared, whose remains
Must be somewhere under us. But because I worried
That I would come up too fast, which can be fatal.
Your lungs can just explode. Instead, I snorkeled
Or swam with my face down in the welcoming water
Looking at the different blues, made all the more
Vivid by the light that seeped through the surface.

And then I turned to float and look at the sky
That was pale and washed, as though it had been
Too long underwater. The boat was in easy reach,
So there was really nothing to worry about, nothing
To suggest disaster, except the waves themselves,
The swell that is unnatural even at the best of times,
All highs and lows, untrustworthy even when calm,
Just undulating willfulness, no conscience, no regrets.

TWO GRECOS

There was a fierce storm in the night,
The sea lunging at us, slapping on stone.
She slept to the beat of that
In the old bed, the mattress stuffed with wool.
Nothing disturbed her except soft sounds.
With the creaking of stairs or pages turning,
The pulling back of sheets or a half sigh,
She woke in hard fright and came
Downstairs to find out what the racket was.
Thunder comforted her, made her yawn.

That night when old Casas and mad Rusinyol
And the young crew that hung around the bar
Brought the Grecos to the town,
I warned her that there might be noise.
I sold them beer sometimes and knew them all.
And they walked quietly like it was God
Was calling out to be restored, having
Been found rotting in an old shop.
Nothing could save us now. The sound of feet
Drove her to the window, mad, roaring
At the neighbours and civil guards to help.

THUNDER ALL NIGHT

I have left it out: the beauty
Of slight things gathered and cast off.
You will drive through the night
On the road from Lleida to La Seu.

Coils and wire untrapped in time.
In time. Rivers squandered mud.
There will be marches and protests
Against the fierce gleam of the proven self.

There is no boat to carry us away.
A small rock, untidy, masculine
Stretches, falls. The wheels crunch and splutter.
I am longing for too much.

FROM THE CATALAN

It was a place we came to then,
Cluttered and forgiving. There were no dead.
One canal, the water fast-flowing, whipped-up.
There was a line of trees.

I will take you into the nest of self.
Before the tree-line, hear me out.
I wish it had not come to this.
Their hands like money, uncomprehending.

Shelter in the vein of stone.
Wisdom has strange, green echoes.
There was something I lost that time
Over there beyond the crowd that gathered.

HIGH UP
(i.m. Bernard Loughlin)

Between the lark and the lammergeyer is the uncrowded sky.
And in the savage brightness a scops owl imagines its own night,
More desperate than the harmless one that
Must come. The earth is terrace and hard ground.

House martins flit as shadows lengthen.
They are all utterance. Soon, they will be gone.
And the sun's round mouth will shut tight
Against the dark.

In the distance, the headlights of a car approach,
Shine with a purpose that hardly
Matters against the strength of things,
And then it matters more than anyone supposed.

AUGUST

One more day to tease us.
I am ready by then. Cherries
Are out of season. Soon
Peaches and nectarines too.

Line of sun moving, until
Its light is all exposure, and
It is time to move indoors
But lazily, like dust in shade.

Then the warning note that sounded
When she came here. Her voice with all
The years, the sweet knowledge, but not
Enough to be prepared.

ANTON WEBERN IN BARCELONA

19 April 1936

Some who have faded approach this uncertain place,
Asking not for shelter, or news of friends,
But tentatively telling whoever is in control
That the conductor, in sadness, knows the score,

Has walked the streets, listening to April noises,
The swifts back in the city, swimming in the air,
Troops gathering, as though summoned by the season,
Players awaiting command, the audience still outside.

OBJECT ON A TABLE

Against the hardness of light, it travels
A distance. There was a time years
Ago when there was only darkness.
Memory walks towards us, half beckoning.

The house is sold; the Folly River's dry.
A strange glistening fire on the horizon
And the lovely warm earth, reddened by use,
Combined to find us wary once the twilight came.

ORCHARD

Then there was peace in Wexford, some cars
In the distance the sole night noise.
We were moving slyly towards the trees,
Soundlessly shifting among brambles and briars.

Windows fading out into the dark
Belonged to unimagined space.
Nothing grew easily here, the gnarled
Half tended back of somewhere. When

Branches gave, she must have heard and stirred.
The wet night earth smelled rank and sour.
Sound of a lock pulled back, a key being turned.
Followed by stillness now the years have gone.

CUSH GAP, 2007

All night the sea-wind makes clear
Its deep antipathy to this house
Whose foundations I will steer
Tomorrow on a different course.

MORNING

I have been telling you this for days.
Sea light and the glow of what is open.
The traffic has been held up. Now go.

If there is a principle at work
In the lovely age-old systems we apply,
I study it. There is too much to regret

And no sweetness in the heavens' air.
One, one, one. The sound fine-tuned,
The end of something, taut, exact.

OPEN HOUSE

This is where they lived; only the old woman is left.
The realtor takes the measure of those who come.
One stray object would ruin the show: a single shoe
Under a bed, or an old toothbrush in the bathroom.

This is where they were happy, the ones who are gone.
Their clothes have been taken away, as well as crumpled
Tubes of sun-tan lotion, pills beyond their sell-by date,
Condoms not needed now, cold cream, insect repellent.

Life and time, the original realtors, make us feel
That all is change and flow; one family has its day
And another buys the house. The shadow that flitted on the wall
And scared the children will rise again to scare some more.

But the vinyl records are gone and will not come back.
The famous lasagna she cooked is history now,
And there was a bird who outdid all his friends one year,
Keeping the house awake. He – if it was a he – is toast.

As you depart, you notice the old woman sitting in an armchair.
Frail, except for her eyes. This was her room, her realm.
The house is open. She supervises all that has been lost.
What the woman sees are sharp, clear things,

Which window picked up dawn light, what names were being called
When silence struck, how life and time seem vivid as they fade.

BLUE SHUTTERS

There were three shutters painted blue
And they gave on to the street
From the first floor of the long
Building. In the July afternoon, when closed,
They unsettled shapes and textures,
Made things seem muted, unfinished, withheld.
Some family waited in the living room.

From that room, a curved stairway led
To a windowless landing. The second
Room to the right, overlooking
The courtyard, was the room where she died,
If died is not too strong a word.
We stayed with her in any case, were quiet
For a while, and then went down

And told the others what had just transpired.
I called the undertaker, shook someone's
Hand, then crept up the stairs again
To find the body covered with a sheet
To protect her, I suppose, making clear
That this was where she was, had been.
It helped to keep her private and at peace.

SHADOWS

In the corner of the room as you lay dead
The old patterned jug rested in its place.
And as the day wore on, the unspeaking
Shadows came, bringing in their wake
Ambiguous claims on the softening air.

You were smiling, almost. The small battle
Between shade and light made the jug's pattern
Blurred and vague, although it must have stayed
The same; it was you who began to change.
Soon they found you and then took you here.

THE MARL HOLE

The waterhens nesting nearby
Seem to like the place; they swim as best
They can, then veer to the edge, waddling
Quietly off. The bottom is muddy, soft clay.
If you made the mistake of wading in
You'd sink through centuries of marl.
There are no fish, except perhaps
Some lazy things, with hardly any eyes.
The lighthouse whistles and the lightship
Whirls. My parents are asleep. I'm lying
In the dark, the softness gathering over me.
It curls, like the night air itself,
Released from the prison of outside,
Tender, persistent, nosing around.

THE NUN

i.

My brother asked if nuns
Wore shoes. And so began
A discussion about nuns

Until someone had the idea,
When my brother left the room,
That my mother should dress

Up as a nun
And pretend to call on us.
She found black clothes

Upstairs and black shoes
And a veil.
She put on glasses

And sneaked out of the house
With her habit on,
Before my brother saw her.

It was after dark. When she
Knocked on the door, it was
A surprise. Nuns did not

Often visit houses
Alone and so late.
She was invited

Into the sitting room, and
We assembled to be introduced
To her. Practical and pleasant,

Like many nuns,
And suitably demure,
She said little at first,

But agreed to have tea, stating
That she was delighted to meet
Us all, and it was so

Nice to be back from the missions.
My brother, who must have been five,
Watched her with interest.

It was clear that she reminded him
Of someone. But he said nothing.
Later, it was agreed that my mother

And all of us had let the joke
Go on for too long.
It was meant to last just

A minute, and then there
Would be a laugh.
But no one knew how to stop it.

My brother moved closer
To her, as we looked on.
But since she was

A visitor, he did not feel
Free to interrupt her
Or indeed touch her

To make sure that she was
Who she said she was.
Or was she someone else?

ii.

When my mother and my brother
Died within a few years of each other,
I did not think of that story.

It only came to me today
Strangely, for no reason.
I can do nothing with it.

There is no relationship
Between that night
And the endless night

In which they live now,
Where we will soon follow.
Then, it was ordinary.

Now, even though they are
In the same grave, they would
Not recognize each other.

The last time I saw them
They were both dressed up,
But it was for good.

In life, however, that time,
The mystery was soon solved.
My mother declared her true self

And took off her glasses
And her veil
And removed the holy look

And soon we got ready for bed,
And then the next day begins.
I cannot connect that image

Of her in disguise
And him amazed that she was
Not a nun at all

With anything other than
The fact that we were there,
In that room, at that time,

Like a photograph of ourselves,
My mother back to normal,
The veil held softly in her hand,

And everyone privately hoping
That no more nuns might come
For a while to the house.

THE ROSARY

I was hitch-hiking
From Gorey back to Enniscorthy
One Sunday night in summer.
I had been drinking vodka,
And was a bit surprised when
The family who picked me up
Said the Rosary, mystery
By mystery, one leading,
The rest following.

The car drove south to the sound
Of sober prayer: One Our Father
Ten Hail Marys, One Glory Be.
To be repeated five times
(The Rosary is repetitious)
And then comes the Hail Holy Queen.
By then we were past Ferns.
It would not be long
Before we reached Enniscorthy.

VINEGAR HILL

The town reservoir on the hill
Was built in the forties.
If you lifted a round metal covering
And dropped a stone, you could

Hear it plonk into the depths.
There were small hollows in the rocks
That, no matter how dry the weather,
Were filled with rainwater.

These rock-pools must have been here
With different water in them
That summer when the rebels
Fled towards Needham's Gap.

From the hill, as the croppies did,
You can view the town, narrow
Streets even narrower, and more
Trees and gardens than you imagined.

It was burning then, of course,
But now, it is quiet. There is,
In the Market Square, a monument
To Father Murphy and the Croppy Boy.

We can see the hill from our house.
It is solid rock in the mornings
As the sun appears from just behind it.
It changes as the day does.

My mother is taking art classes
And, thinking it natural to make
The hill her focal point,
Is trying to paint it.

What colour is Vinegar Hill?
How does it rise above the town?
It is humped as much as round.
There is no point in invoking

History. The hill is above all that,
Intractable, unknowable, serene.
It is in shade, then in light,
And often caught between

When the blue becomes grey
And fades more, the green glistens,
And then not so much. The rock also
Glints in the afternoon light

That dwindles, making the glint disappear.
Then there is the small matter of clouds
That make tracks over the hill in a smoke
Of white as though instructed

By their superiors to break camp.
They change their shape, crouch down
Stay still, all camouflage, dreamy,
Lost, with no strategy to speak of,

Yet resigned to the inevitable:
When the wind comes for them, they will retreat.
Until this time, they are surrounded by sky
And can, as yet, envisage no way out.

BISHOPS

In Enniscorthy cathedral
There are scrolls
Near the altar

On two opposite pillars
That list the names
Of all the bishops

Of Ferns since bishops
Began. Local names,
Latin names, weird

Names. No bishop
Could imagine who
Was coming next,

Or how time
Would pass
And their names

That meant so much
Would soon be followed by names
That meant nothing yet.

Their sermons would also
Be forgotten, prayers too,
And hopes for preferment

That all bishops carry
Humbly in their hearts
– the call to Rome –

Turned to dust.
Nothing much has changed:
There are still bells

And bread and wine,
And body and blood,
And the faithful

(Although smaller in number),
And vestments,
But *Hic est enim corpus meum*

Is now: *This is my body,*
Like a Motown song
Belted out with passion by

Diana Ross and the Supremes
With the Temptations in tow,
As well as something

Intoned in Enniscorthy
Cathedral on a Sunday morning,
The bowed heads,

The bishops' names descending,
And outside,
The light of day

Holding firm against change
At least for the moment
As the church has done

For much of its history
Even as Latin moved
To English

And each bishop
On the scroll made way
For the next one.

KENNEDY IN WEXFORD

There has always been a rumour that the local Bishop
Died the day before Kennedy came to Wexford
In June 1963. There was a feeling, rightly,
That the death would put a damper on the whole occasion.

People might mourn the Bishop or praise the President,
But they could hardly do both on the same day,
So the announcement of the death was postponed,
Until Kennedy had left. A good few must have known,

But they kept quiet on the matter. I have often wondered
If the very prospect of the visit did not, in fact, kill the Bishop.
Perhaps it affected his nervous system. Or froze his heart.
In any case, he lay there undead and unalive, virtual,

His episcopal soul in suspension, like Schrödinger's cat,
Until Kennedy had waved at us all and departed.
Unlike Kennedy, the Bishop was a good-living, pious man.
He wrote a pamphlet on 'The Christian Home' and caused

No fuss until his untimely end. So, once the coast was clear,
You can be sure he went straight to heaven. Yet despite all this,
I believe that if people had been asked to choose between
A dead bishop and a live President, they would have opted for

The latter. I was only eight, but I too would have cheered
For Kennedy. I had been taken out of school and liked
Excitement. We stood on the quays and waited for his car
And went home with news of his suntan and his teeth.

VATICAN II

It was decided
That nuns should be
Let drive.

Such excitement
In the convents!
But the Pope,

Although infallible,
Did not specify
Who precisely

Should do the driving.
This was strange
Since the church

Was aware,
From long experience,
That the devil

Is in the detail.
And now, despite this,
The nuns were left

To work out
For themselves
Who got to drive.

Compared to the other
Changes, like the end
Of the Latin mass

And the turning around
Of the altar, it was
a small thing.

In the end, the Mother
Superiors elected that they
Themselves should be

At the wheel. In the back,
The young nuns would know
Not to criticize.

The clutch, first gear,
The footbrake, the hand-
Brake were too much,

However,
For the old nuns.
With four other nuns

On board, they knew
How to start the car,
Or almost did.

But what then?
The gears! Which gear?
The handbrake! But when?

And then the car
Would shudder until
By some miracle

It was put in the right
Gear and begin to inch
Forward.

It was harder than faith,
Or keeping the vows
Of poverty, chastity

And obedience.
Or living in close
Proximity

To other nuns,
Whispering decades of
The Rosary

Over actual decades
And then more decades
Until the hand

Grew shaky and the sight
Weak and then the dread
Of Sunday afternoons

When they would set out,
Putting the fear of God
Into other users of the road.

No amount of prayer
Could teach Mother Superior
To use the clutch

She would grind the gears,
The car in convulsions,
With the faithful

Looking on,
Glad that the church
Had decided to modernize,

But sorry that
The Vatican didn't think
To issue an order

Urbi et Orbi
That it was the young nuns
Who should be at the wheel.

FACE

Drawn chalk-yellow out of dust
Keeping us free from sin.
There are shadows, sublime inventions
While I listen and say that I too

Have seen visions, skin crack,
The fist banging helplessly on a shut
Door. Locked hollow spaces
Left there after the war.

FROM THE AIR

There was, I know, some hatred before heating
Came. I can see spots, shapes, mounds,
Twisted, left-over. A crash, of course,

Would slice us in two. And then
On the water I saw – no one else
Noticed it – a piece of symmetry swim away.

Nothing else much. Some faint sounds; and the land
For sale; some dark books and humming
In the margins. And the old echoing moon

That goes without saying.

THE TORTURER'S ART

The art he favours has a hint of risk.
A naked bottom, some Cubist forms, but more
Unwieldly, more Picasso than Juan Gris.

Under the sweetness of his homely gaze,
The paintings conform. Nothing white,
Nothing withheld or pale. Instead,

A mess of squiggles, a maze
Of marks and dots, a wildness in the paint,
A love of gesture, filling every space.

The lopsided look of one depicted face
Suggests the torturer does not fear pain
Or wants it just enough to make its mark.

In his house, as guests, we sip and smile.
He dealt with those he needed to defeat.
Freed, he bows and caters for our needs.

AMERICAN POEM

Hedi thinks
I am
middle of the road.
But who
will tell
him
that today
when I had
a token
for one paperback
at McNally
Jackson
I picked
'Not Me'
by Eileen Myles?
At the register
for one second
when the assistant
looked at the
book and
then at
me
I felt like
the most cutting
edge guy
in all New York
and some of
New Jersey,
not to speak of
Connecticut,
and then –

what could I do? –
I went
back to my
road and
I lay down
right on
the broken line
with my arms
outstretched.

Gerard Manley Hopkins Visits the Studio of John Butler Yeats, Dublin, November 1885

November light. From the window it might be a summer sky,
But, in St. Stephen's Green, the shadows make clear
They will come for us before long. No one wants me;
I serve no purpose. At night, I kneel and bow my head and pray.
Meanwhile, there is nothing: a bleak bedroom, a long winter
Ahead and many examination papers in Greek to be graded.
I am like the city itself, half-toned, dull, in-between,
Left out in bad weather. Vexatious and a nuisance,
Too earnest in my pleadings, my mind jaded, my words knotted.

Yeats had the sharp eye of a painter. And, strangely,
Liked the talk of Oxford and the English poets.
I could not, of course, tell him about my efforts,
The poems I wrote. I would like to say that he saw in me
What others missed. And for one second he almost did.
If only he had stopped talking and paid more attention!
But the moment passed. They gossip too much, all of them here.
If Apollo came to Dublin, he would grow garrulous too,
And join their tedious disputes on the merits of Home Rule.

Yeats's gaze was like one of the chances that come in poem-
Making to create two final lines that read like fact.
I had been seeking to say something that is true, just that,
Perhaps something that was known all along, but never
Set down before in words. In the room also was another Jesuit
And the poet Katharine Tynan. Could I dare to tell them
That I still seek that chance, even though my words
Are tortured and contrived? And I am, of course, afraid.
The conversation became quiet and the light subdued.

Yeats asked me what I thought life was. He had that Irish look,
Earnest and mocking at the same time, until his face
Changed. He said, surely I must know what life meant?
It is an ordeal, I said. It is a path. He shook his head.
No, I mean life, not its opposite. What is the game of life?
I don't call it a game, I told him. It is a place where we
Purify our souls, but never enough. But life! he said. Life!
He looked at Katharine Tynan and my fellow priest as though
They might know what it means for us to be on earth.

His eyes were bright with argument. She too lit up, the poet,
And spoke of some sacred place on the western seaboard.
I wanted to ask her later what it was called, but I forgot.
Instead, I saw Yeats the painter in the time to come,
His face thinner but the same flash in his eyes,
A brush in his hand, a canvas in front of him
That had been scraped down. The outline still on the surface
Was himself as artist, brush in hand, ready to start again,
Half-animal in his willingness to pounce, half-spirit too.

I am at three removes – English in Ireland, a convert
To the Roman Church, a poet who is not in print.
They must have spoken of that after my departure.
But at the door, as I took one glance at Yeats, I saw
His face cloud over and then break into an artful smile.
I am not certain, but it looked as if a guarded radiance
Had come to him like grace. He was all shine. Then I left.
Since the Green was locked, I walked back around the railings
To the house, glad, despite my innocence, that I knew the way.

DUBLIN: SATURDAY, 23 MAY, 2015

The years of excitement had gone.
They were almost sixty now; both lived alone.
They texted each other sometimes
And met mid-week in a quiet bar.

Once or twice in the days of Minsky's
Or in a sauna called The Gym
They had got together.
But it didn't mean much. It made them friends.

But what to do now that gay marriage had been
Voted for by the Irish people?
That Saturday, they met for lunch
In a new café in Phibsboro

And afterwards walked via Berkeley Street
And Blessington Street to O'Connell Street
And then to Dublin Castle where they
Found the crowd already assembled in the Yard,

All brightly smiling, all in groups,
Cheering for this new-found freedom.
There were more lesbians than they expected
And they were used to the fact that

At gay events now the guys were young.
Anyone middle-aged had retreated
As though in shame to the suburbs,
Learning to take things slow,

The gay past coming to life only
When they spotted someone from the old days
On a street in the city centre
And gave a brusque nod and passed on.

On a platform there were politicians
And speeches through a bad PA system.
Same-sex couples kissed for the cameras.
'Same sex,' one man said to the other,

'Used to mean that you were fed up
Having the same sex all the time
And went to a park or a public toilet
For a bit of novelty.'

They laughed, but it was no joke.
They knew no one here at all.
They were the only ones bored.
'We could become conspicuous,' one said,

'For being not gay enough.
That is how the world has turned.
The Minister is gay, the Fianna Fáil
Man too, and Ursula Halligan.

And all we can tell them is
That things were not always so.
Hard to imagine now being frightened
To go into Rice's or BD's

And hovering around outside
At closing time, in case
There was a chance. But
There never was. Chances

Came by chance in those years
Like the Friday night in the Manhattan
I got talking to a soldier
And took him home.

Unimaginable the luck the fun!
And both of us sober enough
To go through the night
And into the morning.

No sign of him here. Or the fellow
In the monkey suit in that disco
At the top of the Rathmines Road
That didn't last long.'

'What didn't last long?'
'Neither that guy nor the disco,
But both did the trick that night
When I least expected it.'

Without planning to leave,
They moved out of the Castle Yard
And found themselves in Dame Street.
'I would like us to visit,'

One said, 'some of the places
That are gone now, the ones
We remember, the gay spots
That have fallen off the map.

And no one will remember soon.'
And then they laughed, cheered
By the memory of The Gym, often
Called The Garda Club,

Even though the Guards left it alone,
In Dame Lane, that links The George
To one of the gates
Of Dublin Castle.

The Gym was on two floors, the first
With sauna and whirlpool
And porn den and coffee shop,
And little private rooms upstairs.

At the weekend it was open
Twenty-four hours so fellows
Could come up from the country
And move in, ordering toasted

Sandwiches to keep them going,
Sleeping a bit and then wandering
Like hunters through the thicket
Of who might be available.

It was almost sad, but then
It wasn't. In the silence of
Those cubicles upstairs, what
Had been dreamed of happened.

'Do you remember,' one of them asked,
'The judge who appeared
Naked when the rest of us wore towels.
I spent time in the dark with him once

To see what he was like.'
'What was he like?'
'He was quick about it, but
He wanted it more than anyone I have

Ever known. One fellow boasted
That at the end of their session
He said "Thank you, my lord",
But I pretended I did not know

Who he was. It was his own business.'
'He has gone to the sweet sauna in the sky.'
'He has been welcomed there with open arms.
Funny, in The Gym I remember the watching

And waiting, more than the action itself.
I should have kept a diary.'
They walked up George's Street
Towards where Bartley Dunne's pub was,

So glamorous in those days.
'The first time I went in
I saw all these people talking,
Like it was normal to be there.

I couldn't wait to go home.
I thought I could meet someone
In one second and sneak
Out the door to safety.

But there was no safety, then.'
'At work, there was a young guy
Who used to go there
With his friends and watch

All the old queens, as he called us,
Go crazy for him,
Tongues hanging out,
And all of his friends laughing.'

They walked to the corner
Of Stephen's Green
And South King Street,
The entrance to the Centre,

Busy with Saturday shoppers.
This was once the site
Of Rice's pub, the front bar
Gay, the rest for everyone.

'Do you remember Brian's funeral?'
Silence. Then: 'They wouldn't
Let them have an open coffin
Because it was AIDS.'

'There were fellows went home
To die. You never saw them again.
Just realized gradually
That they'd gone from the scene.'

They grew quiet then
At the thought of that time.
And looked around
For any distraction.

They spoke of getting a taxi
To Palmerston Park,
Once a cruising ground
Both by day and at night,

Or to the Phoenix Park.
Or walking to Adelaide Road
To the site of the gents' toilet
Now demolished.

'That toilet was busy
On Sunday afternoons.
I never knew why, much busier
Than the toilets on Burgh Quay,

Gone too, gone the way
Of many gents toilets.
There was another toilet
Near Westland Row,

But that was before my time.'
'What about the one at
The 10 bus stop on
Infirmary Road?

Or the one just across the road
In Stephen's Green.
Or the Meeting of the Waters
At the Thomas Moore statue

At College Green.'
They walked down Grafton Street.
'Did you ever get lucky here?'
'Never once! It was a safe space

For straight people. As soon
As they set foot in the street
Gay people took on the guise
Of straight people.

Wicklow Street was different,
But not very different.'
They thought about
The Hirschfeld Centre

And the dances there
On a Sunday night.
And meetings mid-week
About our rights.

'Did you ever go to the other
Saunas? Like Incognito or The Dock,
Or the one on Parnell Square?
Dublin was one big sauna then.'

'I tried them all.
Secret spaces, with their own
Rules, like The Matrix,
Or an underworld,

Grown men as ghosts,
And rooms beyond rooms,
It was crepuscular and then
Suddenly bright.

And it was always hard to know
When to leave.
Departure felt like defeat.
The Dublin night

Was unforgiving if you were
A man walking alone.
I liked all the new places –
The Boilerhouse

And Pantibar and the Dragon
And the Front Lounge
But I kept away from the George,

And then, over one long winter,

I kept away from them all
And never went back.
Got married to my right hand.'
They veered into Suffolk Street

And then back to Dame Street
Towards Dublin Castle,
Expecting to see supporters
Of the referendum on the street

With banners or with
Funny haircuts. But even
As they approached the bank
And then City Hall itself

Dublin looked normal
And that gave them some
Satisfaction. Secretly,
They had worried that life

Would hone its skills
At mocking them
For how they had lived.
The past was all over

And memories would fade.
The city would become a map
Of another city

That only they could read.

From Parliament Street,
They crossed the river,
Deciding to take
The slow way home.

They'd text each other soon
And meet in a quiet bar.

GELLERT BATHS, SPRING 1990

I have not been here since I met you last,
The guy said, in his perfect English.
We wallowed in the sulphury water.
Back in his place, I learned something new:
If you pour sparkling wine onto an erect cock,
The bubbles stay there for a while, even if
The champagne wets the floor. This means
That when I kneel to suck this Hungarian's dick,
To my great delight, I discover that my mouth
      Is soon alive with bubbles.

DEAD CINEMAS

i.

Dublin is a map
Of dead cinemas, once
Darkened spaces now
Demolished, made into
Shops or just closed up.

The Grafton, where I saw
'Love in the Afternoon',
And wondered if Bernard
Verley was right not to do
What he did not do.

The Astor, where one Friday
At the early evening show
I saw 'Cries and Whispers'
And screamed out loud
When she cut herself.

The Academy in Pearse Street,
Where I saw 'Amarcord',
Or most of it, since
The censor scissored out
The whole wanking scene.

The world is divided:
Men and women; black and white;
Rich and poor; and those who
Go to the cinema alone
And those who do not.

In the Regent, on my own,
I saw 'The Deerhunter'
And 'Halloween II'. It was
A bad period made worse
By going to those two films.

The International had the grace
To become the IFC,
Where I saw 'The Stepford Wives'
And 'Salò'. It eventually became
The Sugar Club.

In the Green Cinema, I saw
'The Great Gatsby', with
Robert Redford and Mia Farrow
But did not believe a single
Shot in the whole fiasco.

In the Screen opposite Trinity
Over a whole weekend
In the company of Mary Holland
I saw all of 'Heimat'; it started
Good, then fell apart slightly.

In Abbey Street, below
The Adelphi, there was
A small cinema where late
One Sunday night
In the winter of 1975

I saw Polanski's 'Repulsion'
Which was not as frightening
As the walk back home to
Hatch Street, with Dublin
Damp, emptied out.

Soon, there were art films
And other films; the former
Did not have ads for
McDowell's Happy Ring House
And were more solemn generally.

In the end I stopped
Going much because
I found it hard
Facing back out
Into the world.

ii.

At night and for much of the day
These spaces were empty
And this must have given
Them an intimation
What it would be like

When they were not there at all,
Just openings in our dreams,
Ways of getting through
Friday night and Saturday
In the time before

Gas central heating
And, of course, before
VHS and DVD
And streaming services
And the dimming of the faculties.

But enough of them still in place
To hear echoes of the Bach cello
In 'Cries and Whispers' as I cross
O'Connell Street Bridge,
Or see Verley's blue pullover

On Grafton Street, imagining
Pearse Street, nostalgic
For the wanking scene
In 'Amarcord' that I never saw,
Hearing Mia Farrow whisper

On Stephen's Green,
Or noticing the cracks in the footpath
In 'Repulsion' getting wider,
Opening up
To eat me as I walk home.

VARIATIONS ON A SCENE FROM MAEVE BINCHY

I was sure I might learn something from her.
So, one day, in the car, when Maeve's novel
'Evening Class' was being read out on the radio,
I decided I would listen closely. It was about
A woman who taught Italian in Dublin
And had come to Rome with her adult students.
One night, when she went early to the restaurant
She had booked for the group, she found it closed.
In despair, she wandered in the streets only
To find another restaurant that had just had
A cancellation. So, she took all her students there.
Towards the end of the meal, the owner
Of the place appeared with his wife and brother.
Having looked intently at the Italian teacher,
They approached her, and it slowly emerged
That they were her long-lost family from Sicily
Or somewhere south of Naples. They had given up hope
Of ever finding her, and she had despaired
At the loss of them. And now here they were
In Rome, re-united, all the students watching.
And as they spoke in an Italian that was familiar
And fast, in tones that were warm and relieved,
Indeed delighted, there were free little glasses
Of *Sambuca* for everyone. Life would never be
The same again.

I imagined the woman in the street. She had
Come to Rome, as she did each year, but it
Seemed almost alien now after all the time.
She was no longer used to the city,
Having lived in Dublin for much too long.

Each year, she would go to an aunt in Lecce
Whose phobias were sunlight and seafood,
But that would not be for a few days more.
She had some cousins with whom she had lost touch.
In every restaurant in Rome, even at lunchtime,
They wanted you to have all the courses.
It was too much. She had taken to having a burger
In McDonald's in Piazza di Spagna, but she would
Never share this news with anyone. Also, no one
Wanted a lone diner. She had almost gone into
A restaurant just now, but could not face the waiters
Looking at her with pity. She wondered if it was
Her eyesight, or if the streets-lights really were
More dim. Years ago, she brought a group of students
Here, but they had got drunk on the first night
And kept asking her to take them to another bar.
Only two of them turned up in the morning
For the trip to Villa Borghese, with the tickets
Pre-paid. And they made a joke out of it. She was glad
To be alone.

Or this version: She loves Roman nights, the heat
Held in, released, held in. And likes knowing
That, if strolling from Piazza di Spagna to
Piazza di Popolo, Via Margutta is the best way.
Once night falls, she seems to remember less.
Even the sound of the language from passers-by
Reminds her of nothing really, no childhood
Days, not even parents, sisters, friends. It is a
Language she hardly uses any more, except to teach.
And the fetid smell mixed in with the sound
Of steps against stone and faint television sounds
And cooking smells come to her as news from now,
With no hint of summers past with the heat baking

In the bricks or lizards flitting into cuts in rock.
Soon, it would be a relief to return to Terenure,
To summer drizzle and midges swarming in the long
Back garden. In the restaurant, she knows how to get
A corner table without anyone feeling sorry for her.
She studies the menu. When the waiter comes to tell
Her the list of specials, he stops for a second
And takes her in. She sees some suggestion
In his eyes, perhaps even a resemblance to someone,
But to whom? To some boyfriend a summer long ago?
An uncle, her father? Someone she imagines?
Her brother who died?

Trastevere on a Friday night in June, restaurants
Too crowded, tourists making too much noise.
They pass a small place, just closing up. She says:
Look in there. It was last summer. One of the bigger
Restaurants insisted that they did not have our booking.
It was just a pale excuse for turning us away.
I was in such a rage. And other places were packed out.
And then we stopped outside this little spot here,
And saw a man, he must have been the owner, at the door.
His work was done and he was taking in the air. When we asked
If he had a table, he checked inside, and yes, they had
A table for the four of us at the back, near the kitchen.
We had no reason to be fussy that night! After we
Had finished and we were waiting for the bill, a man
Whom I took to be the son of the owner approached our table.
He studied all of us but then just me, and turned away.
I was signing for the credit card when he came again
And stood watching me, intense, whistling under his breath.
And then he asked if I remembered him. I did not know
What to say. It had been all so long ago. I shook my head,
But not to deny I knew him, rather to make clear

That I could not engage with him now. Now was not
The time. I shook my head again. When we stood up to leave,
He moved closer, whispering: Why did you just go, that time?
A phone call would have done, a letter, a message,
Any word at all.

I RAN AWAY

On this very spot, forty-five years ago,
By the canal between Baggot Street
And Leeson Street, I was attacked
And arrested by four hungry-looking
Members of the Special Branch.
They were hunting down terrorists

And I must have had a suspicious look.
What stays in my memory is a moment
When I was sprinting up to Leeson Street
Bridge with the four plainclothes cops in pursuit
And I passed a prostitute who was alone,
Leaning against the railing. 'You're worse

To run,' she said, her tone stoic, implacable,
Uninvolved. And then later after they
Caught me and pinned me down, the Branchmen
Saw that I had a book with me that might,
I suppose, be helpful in their investigations.
One of them took it up, opened it, and,

As his colleagues asked me questions
About my putative fight for Irish freedom,
The cop flicked through the pages.
Soon, he indicated to one of
The others that he, too, should
Examine these lines of verse, perhaps

They held a buried clue to some vast
Conspiracy against the state itself.
I kept one eye on them as I explained
To their companions that I was an innocent student
'Why did you run when you saw us?' they asked.
'How could I have known,' I asked,

'That you are Branchmen?' He looked as if
I had questioned the essence of his being.
A day later, with my breath back,
I knew I should have explained that I ran
Because within all of us hides a latent guilt
That waits to be woken by Branchmen real or false.

What made me run, though, to tell the truth,
Was that I was simply afraid of my shite.
No point in evoking hidden darknesses,
Or atavistic, primal forms of shame.
Meanwhile, the two Branchmen were still leafing
Through the book, bored and puzzled, it seemed,

By what they found there. They soon indicated
To the other Branchmen that maybe the fellow
They had arrested, likely as he was,
Might not be on the run, and not the type
To give his life for Ireland. It might be wise
To hand him back the book and let him go.

THE HOUSE

Thirty years ago I went to Spain,
Abandoning the Dublin house,
Paying no mortgage, no bills,
For twelve months, aware how easily
The building society could re-possess.

It seemed irresponsible at the time
To risk losing the house
But I wrote a book in Spain
And had a whale of a time there
And was glad I made the choice.

In my mind, I would sometimes track
The dark interior of that house,
The books and papers, the paintings,
The things I had loved and collected
Reduced to objects I no longer missed.

I was the ghost in the corner who made
The sounds that never filled the house,
The cook who made no dinners, after which
No one washed up. Night fell and day came
In the dreamed-of place now out of use.

One mid-December night, back in Dublin and broke,
I tried the key to the door of that old house,
Hoping that they had not changed the lock.
It opened, just about, because piles of post
Were blocking the way, and so I had to push.

No lights, no heating, no phone, many letters
From the Irish Nationwide about the house
And all the arrears that had accrued.
I stood in the darkened emptiness and smiled
At the thought of being home at last.

TWO OR THREE

i.

No matter how old I grow,
The verger at St. Anne's
Stays the same.

He is walking
Along Baggot Street,
Going home.

Most of the singers
And players from that time
Are dead, most

Of the audience even.
On Sunday
Afternoons in spring

Or late winter
We were among the youngest
At those concerts.

Before the hour changed
Dublin was almost
Dark by half past four.

ii.

Two of them shadow me still.
John Beckett, who began
By introducing each cantata,

His tone brisk,
His way of conducting
Almost factual.

(Later, I read that
He disliked
Handel.)

And Bernadette Greevy's
Mezzo voice:
Wo Zwei und Drei

Versammelt sind.
This was Dublin
Then.

The music gathered
Up the pale light
From outside.

By the time
The concert was over
Darkness had mostly fallen.

EMILY KNGWARREYE IN DUBLIN

i.

The world lives in history
While we, poor lost ones,
Wither in time.

The knowledge I can
Bring to this is scant,
The edge of a town,

An enclosed world,
A semi-detached house,
A small front garden,

Some space at the side
And back, a plot
Behind the shed

Where once an apple
Tree did not flourish
Nor the damson tree

Planted in its stead.
Some flowers:
Dahlias, sweet pea,

Lavender. A gooseberry
Bush.
Some grass.

No great desert
In the distance,
No vast sunsets,

No sacred rocks,
No dreaming
To be done,

No ancient language –
Unless maybe English
Or Irish – no sense that

The Slaney, the Urrin,
The Boro, are holy
Rivers whose source

We venerate.
No worship of Bree Hill,
Nor the Blackstairs

Mountains,
Nor Vinegar Hill,
Despite the songs

And the battle.
The few who came
To paint this light

Or write poetry here
Looked for rutted lanes,
Narrow roads,

Briars and brambles,
Windfall-sweetened
Soil.

ii.

The painting sits
Between two windows
In an untidy

Dublin interior.
Its ochre and black
Black stripes

On an ochre ground –
Stand out
Against what is

Tentative, unbrave,
Reticent, raked,
The sky outside

A great withholding.
Bergs of clouds
Blown away

By the embattled
Light, soft
Against sharp,

When it slants
Into this front room
Upstairs at five

And stays long
Enough to unsettle
The piles of books,

The dust,
The day-bed,
The open door.

IN WASHINGTON DC

It is always hard to know what questions to ask:
What was here before all this, maybe, and where
Precisely is the swamp? And in this bookstore
Monica Lewinsky bought which book for Bill Clinton?
Some Trees? Questions of Travel? The Wild Iris?
For the Union Dead? And what did she get in return?

There is a gay bar called 'The Fireplace' which helps
To make us all feel at home. There are people,
I suppose, not too far away, who think this might
Remind us of the fires of hell. But let's not go there.
Nearby, Lindsey Graham and Mitch McConnell are asleep.
And in this city too Jon Ossoff's tucked up in his bed.

Where are the senators of yesteryear, the famous names
Never out of the headlines: Joseph Robinson, Charles
McNary, Hiram Johnson, Francis T. Maloney, David I.
Walsh? The I. must have stood for Ignatius, I suppose.
(I have just looked it up and that is, in fact, the case.)
He died in 1947, being the ninth of ten children.

On the streets downtown, as I stroll at lunchtime,
I could have just passed someone planning to reform
The penal system, or the Proud Boys, who come
Not single spies, or Q himself, or a lobbyist promoting
A bomb able to detect from a distance the disruptive heart
Of an infidel, and also useful at weddings and wakes.

Once, in the other century, the world was run from here.
They fought wars, ran coups and invested heavily
In the infrastructure of bombed-out Europe. In return,
They must have wanted treasure, love or even loyalty.
They did nothing out of the goodness of their hearts.
But they were not all bad. Or so people said at the time.

IN THE WHITE HOUSE

Some guests pushed other guests so they
Could get a better view of the Obamas
And Joe Biden. At one moment, a group
Decided to move right up to the front,
Getting their colleagues to behave
Like security guards creating a safe corridor.

The place was packed with Irish-Americans in suits.
I saw Gabriel Byrne. Obama and Biden had a boyish
Way of telling each other jokes while Michelle
Obama stood apart, unamused. The White House décor
Was fussy, with too many different textures
In the wallpaper, carpets and coverings.

And the paintings were bad. At one moment,
Obama was close to us, but then someone
Got in the way. He was about to depart
When, luckily, Joe Hassett politely called him back
And brought me and Garry Hynes towards him.
Obama's hand was soft when I briefly shook it.

We were ushered then into a large, long room.
And this is the part that remains most memorable:
They left us to enjoy our drinks for a while
And then they decided it was time for us all to go.
But they made no announcement. Instead, the staff
Stood in a line at the back of the room, and moved

One step at a time towards us, letting no one get
Behind them. They did this nonchalantly, casually.
It was gradual, but it was also firm. We were so high
On our brush with fame, however, we hardly noticed,
Until when they were a third of the way towards the exit
And we realized they meant business; we would have to go.

Was this a trick of Nixon's? Was it conjured up by Barbara Bush?
Was it a Jackie special? Was it put in place by the Clintons?
Or was it an Obama original? Anyway, it was clear that
The *céad míle fáilte* and the dear little shamrock meant
Less than nothing now. And, once the staff had hit half-way,
It would not be long before we were all outside the door.

Inside, with us gone, Obama would make decisions.
Outside, we, the disenchanted Irish, hailed taxis, unavailing.
We had expected to learn something in that house about power
And politics. Instead, we witnessed what it is like
To wear your welcome out. It does seem tempting, even still,
To imagine the line of waiters as a metaphor for something,

For soft power, soft coercion, for how to take a firm stance
On foreigners. Or for time's pawlike purposeful intent,
How it moves discreetly, it inches forward without
Us noticing. Just as we are being distracted by wondrous sights
And thoughts and idle talk, it pushes us firmly
Into timeless night and will not let us back.

But that is stretching it. Instead, the thing itself, the fact,
Remains vivid in my mind. It was surprising and exact.
It left us all speechless, unsure if we would ever have
The courage to tell our friends at home in any detail
Of the ingenious and effective scheme used to get us
Out of the White House on St Patrick's Day 2010.

LATE

It is late, and there is little left to say.
Yes, I know that there is a case to be made
For the novels of Pamela Hansford Johnson
Over the novels of Elizabeth Jane Howard.

And if I were to come to earth again,
I would like to be Gerald Ford, who slipped
In and then out of office, and was soon
Overshadowed by his wife Betty and her clinic.

I prefer the Holy Ghost, who never got crucified
Or made the Sermon on the Mount, to God the Father,
Who made too much fuss. His mother would have been
Proud of him, if he ever had a mother, if he was 'he',

If he was a ghost at all, or even holy. I mean,
What did he do? No thunder. No miracles. Maybe
He helped out when he was needed at the conception
Of Jesus. Yes, that might have been his contribution.

I like Dirty Dick Mulcahy, James Dillon, Alan Dukes
And Michael Noonan, leaders of the Fine Gael party
Who never became Taoiseach. What about Tom O'Higgins
Who was ten thousand votes away from being President?

Or R.A. Butler who nearly became Prime Minister,
Who put through the Education Act of 1944, of course,
And died as the fashion of having just initials
Before your name died too. It could mark you out

As Anglo-Catholic in religion, classicist in literature,
And royalist in politics, like T.S. Eliot. Better to be
Called Ted, or Andrew, or Carol Ann, or Simon, the names
Of the last four poet laureates. And maybe better still,

To be the poet laureate that no one at all remembers
And no one at all reads, like Alfred Austin, who lies
In peace. It is late, and I am buried deep in C.P. Snow
And exhausted straddling the two cultures and thinking

Hard about Raymond Williams and F.R. Leavis and J.I.M.
Stewart, who had a nerve. In America, when they attacked
The Capitol, they tore pages from the books of George Rudé,
Books that would have put strange ideas into their heads.

It is too late for thoughts; there's not much time either
For idle musings, odd associations. What is the difference
Between John Wain and John Wayne, I might have asked.
Now, what can I ask? And what would you say in reply?

NOVEMBER IN AMERICA

It is the night of the election,
And even the Republicans in the room
Do not believe Trump can beat Hillary.
A Republican woman tells me
About Obama: You see, he killed a man.

Later, I wondered if there were signs
Then of the catastrophe to come.
And, yes, at the opening of the event
Jessye Norman from her wheelchair sang
'You'll Never Walk Alone', her tone

Grave, stately, like she was singing
High Mass crossed with one of
The sad Schubert songs. The piano
Accompaniment was even more weighty
Than the voice. *When you walk*

Sounded as though we were entering
The dark underworld rather than
The raucous opening of an away
Match, the Liverpool fans belting
The song straight into the goal.

I had to warn my English colleague
That we had somehow to get through
The evening. She was shaking
With laughter. 'I will pinch
You if you don't stop.'

Through a storm. The New Yorkers
Were all silent, like God had been
Invoked or the Nation or the Founding
Fathers themselves had descended and
Were holding their heads on high.

They were not afraid of the dark.
I thought of all the sad stories
I had ever heard to stop myself
Laughing out loud as the voice
Soared to further pitches of pure

Meaningfulness. How moving! How true!
Yes, go on: *at the end of a storm*
There is a golden sky. Soon,
The Republican woman will confide
In me that Mitt Romney knew

For a fact that Obama had killed a man.
If he, honorable leader that he is,
Had not decided to conceal the knowledge
For the sake of the nation,
He could have won in 2012, she says.

Half way through the song, there is
A crisis. People have noticed us,
The Irish one, the Brit. Maybe they think
We are crying at the sadness of it all,
And soon we will be uplifted

By *the sweet silver song of a lark.*
But one or two have spotted that
We are actually laughing as Jessye
Wrings her hands and allows a quaver
To carousel unbearably into her voice:

Walk on through the wind.
How could that be funny? It is
The story of struggle against
Adversity. Becoming great again,
Despite it all. Later,

I will find out that my friend
The Republican woman is married to
One of the richest guys in New York
And that Steve Mnuchin is at the table,
But just now as the singer walks on

Through the rain, there is not
A dry eye among the Americans,
Through their dreams be tossed and blown.
I am sore with laughter and the Brit
Is as sick as a parrot, as they say.

That night, there is hope in
Their Yankee hearts, as the ballots
Are being guarded against the truth.
Soon, twitter, fake news and rage itself
Will be all the rage, and

Children will be held in cages.
And dreams will be tossed and blown.
But that night we see them in all
Their innocence, loving the song
And comforted by the singer.

Walk on, walk on. Outside it was
November in America. We went to a bar.
There was hope – some hope – in the hearts
Of those poised for power. It is sobering
To remember we were not laughing anymore.

LINES WRITTEN AFTER THE SECOND MODERNA VACCINE AT DODGERS' STADIUM LOS ANGELES, 27 FEBRUARY 2021

I am a shining example
I am the Lord, thy God
I am Gavin Newsom
I am Gavin Friday
I am Gavin O'Reilly
I am Lorraine Hunt Lieberson
I am Mullingar
I am the Junior Senator for Nebraska
I am the Boys of Wexford
I am Mikis Theodorakis
I am passing through Ballindaggin
I am one of the Byrnes of Ferns
I am a poor wayfaring stranger
I am red with honesty
I am Sligo Rovers
I am Sinéad Bean de Valera
I am purple with despair
I am Nana Mouskouri
I am green with senseless passion
I am Christina Onassis
I am Wicklow County Council
I am a man of constant sorrow
I am Yves Bonnefoy
I am The San Francisco Chronicle
I am a big ignorant rugby-player
I am Evonne Goolagong (Cawley)
I am Edwin Arlington Robinson
I am the boy in the back of the bus
I am Le Corbusier

I am the Evening Herald
I am Alice Munro
I am Alice Ben Bolt
I am Casper Goodwood
I am Ben Dunne Junior
I am Ben Dunne Senior
I am the Shelbourne Hotel Horseshoe Bar
I am Willa Cather
I am a gnat, a gnu, a gnome, a gnit
I am a big lump of Camembert
I am a Coveney from Cork
I am Henry Moore
I am Whelahan's of Finglas
I am Norwegian
I am never going Ryanair again
I am the Colleen Bawn
I am Flahavan's Porridge Oats
I am the Ginger Man
I am Declan Kiberd
I am Merrick Garland
I am a tin of golden syrup
I am the Central Catholic Library
I am Somerville and Ross
I am half a crown
I am the Lass of Aughrim
I am Allen (Bader) Ginsberg
I am Betty Ruth
I am Lawrence Ferlinghetti
I am the boy in the bubble
I am back in business
I am speaking to all parties
I am St. Joseph of Cupertino
I am the cat's pyjamas
I am W.B. Yeats

DECEMBER

I wondered that December day
What I would miss. December light:
The air liquid and grey
An hour before the ambiguous hour.

Time when the mind's half-filled with dreams.
The gift of pure dazzling consciousness.
Some books. And music, not to be heard again.
The touch of flesh, your hand.

When I first heard talk of death
I was eight, just in from school,
And my mother, staring in the mirror, said
That my father would die, and soon he did.

From then I did not put my trust
In anything much. When I summon up the names
Of ones I love, for example, I recoil
At having to whisper what has remained unsaid.

TWO PLUS ONE

My heart is watching and weakening
Mercilessly counting the beats;
It is bored, casually waiting
For this to cease.

My father died at fifty-three.
Vessels leaked in his brain.
Then arteries weakened.
He moaned in pain.

My mother's eyes were grey as his
Were blue. Her breath
Rose high over the town
Before it sank in death.

I have their two weak hearts in one
Weak heart, their eyes merged in my gaze.
His slow smile, her soft side-glance
Oversee my days.

IN MEMORIAM

Her friends are coming up the hill.
She sits in her easy chair
And talks as though the evening will
Dim gently as the dimming fire.

Outside there is a wooden box
Where she will lie until time ends.
Now we hear some mourners' knocks
And they come in and night descends.

Slowly, we lift her from her place
And lead her to the crowded hall.
We put her firmly in the case,
Nail down the top once and for all.

RITUAL

The upper air is sweet, celestial.
But why should that bother us below
Where the noise of the world is muffled
Drum sound and last night's wind and rain?
Yes, the woman sings; her song
Will be used to waken the heavens
When the chance comes, but it might never.

In the book that points the way,
I found words and signs that served only
To mystify me further. It is not easy
For anyone being in the world,
And yet I remember how fiercely he held
On to life, struggling for one more
Gasp, his eyes tenacious in his head.

Hard to know what to call it:
Ritual, maybe, or ordeal, like
The children's mass at five o'clock
On Holy Thursday in Enniscorthy.
And although the search is for completion,
It is not death; it opens rather
Into brightness, soundlessness.

FATHER & SON

They took him to beyond Davidstown,
Stopped the car on a side-road until
There was no sign of anyone. And then,
To get his cords working again,
He was to shout at the top of his voice.
The more he tried to do it, though,
The more it came out as pain, a soft howl.

The other one lost his control of speech
In the same season. Hard consonants
Defeated him. It was as if a door
Was locked and he was in a room
Banging, but unable to call out, and from
The other side a sound came, faint at first,
Then familiar, almost clear: pain, a soft howl.

IN SAN CLEMENTE

Dripping water and the smell of darkness.
This is where I will go. Follow me now.

Time pressed down, led down,
Down as the steps lead down.
I will go into the dark without you.

Below this below there is more
And it is below that I belong to.
Don't follow me further. Move away.
Don't follow me further.

ECCLES STREET

No dreams, or
Anything like that.
Sharp listening

For sounds in
The corridor,
Night noises.

I am awake
When the oncologist
Visits between six

And seven.
When he leaves,
Anything at all

Swims into the room:
A marinade I never had,
Someone from UCD

I'd half forgotten,
A poem by Thomas Campion,
Monteverdi's *Beatus Vir*.

ii.

This is the Mater Private
In Eccles Street.
On this very site,

Before the nuns
Demolished the building,
The Blooms once lived.

Molly and Leopold
And their daughter
Milly.

iii.

If the chemo
Zaps the tumour
And doesn't kill me

I am going to have
An exemplary morning.
I will make you

Breakfast in bed,
Toast and slices
Of liver

With grilled mutton
Kidneys, and tea.
I will go

Around the corner
To the shop in
Dorset Street.

And when I come back
I will pick up
Letters from

The floor
That have just
Been delivered.

And then the day ahead,
The epic day,
Will begin.

iv.

Who is in the next room?
Strange all week
To see

Heavy-metal
Guys, some bald
With bellies

And big beards,
Strut bravely
To visit that room.

Yesterday
Even more of them came.
And then it began,

The music, someone
On an electric guitar,
The chords filled with

Tough life,
Unforgiving sound,
And loud.

This was music
From the world
Zinging through the ward.

I found out that
The patient had permission
For this,

The loudness must
Have reminded him
Of a time when no one

Had any reason to worry
About anything.
Defiant sound

Ripping the air
In our zone of tubes
And cotton wool,

Each of us watching
The doctor's face
For news

When he re-appears
In our rooms
At first light.

v.

No ghosts lurk here.
The room has been sanitized
Against hospital bugs

As much as against
The transmigration
Of souls.

I prefer
Getting the chemo
In my left arm.

It does not make
A sound,
The liquid.

It might as well
Be Lucozade,
Or Twinings' nectar tea.

vi.

In the dream world
There is a funeral
And a walk

Up Westland Row.
I could easily
Lose my own keys

If the steroids
Were nor thumping
Through me,

Causing me,
By the afternoon,
To forget nothing.

What would it
Mean to go into
The National Library,

Where the same readers
Are at the same desks
Since 1973

Or so I see
As I look around?
Funny how resonant

The sound of the turning
On and off
Of the little light-switch

On each desk in the library
Becomes
In this hospital room

Without resonant sound.
Why has that little
Snap-sound grown to be

What is holding
Me together as
The juice flows?

vii.

What would the nurses
Say, if I got out of bed
And put on

My dressing-gown
And slippers
And made

My way by bus or taxi
Or on foot to Davy Byrnes
For gorgonzola

And wine,
And some ineluctable
Modality of the visible?

And if I ended the
Night with some
Young poet,

Talking shite in a dive
Down the quays
Before taking him home,

And making breakfast
Again, ready
For another round?

Orpheus came to this house
On an August Bank Holiday weekend.
He made no fuss; it was as if
I had called a plumber, or a man

To fix the roof. From the roof,
He could expand his horizons –
Raven Point to the south;
Rosslare Harbour; Tuskar Rock

Holding its breath in the light.
When Orpheus pushed the open door
Flicked through the CDs,
Fumbled with the sound system,

And put on *Das Lied von der Erde* –
The Kathleen Ferrier version –
I could have told him what it
Would do to the room.

The woodwind holds back
And soars again, knowing
That her voice will break up
Whatever peace there was here.

Orpheus will go to the cliff
And call the dead to come
To us from the sea where
They have been swimming.

He will promise my mother
The music. But she is checking
The water, to see how cold it is,
Then wading out before turning

And giving me a look,
Dismissive, distant,
And then floating away,
Unenticèd by the song.

SMALL WONDER

I am in Venice during the pandemic,
Here to pay homage to aftermath,
Afterthought, to what hardly matters.
I shrug as I pass the Bridge of Sighs
And will not go near Piazza San Marco
Which is deserted anyway, unused.
Gondoliers stand idle at minor bridges.
No one is sailing up and down
The Grand Canal or standing in the Frari
Staring in awe at Titian's Assumption.

I am looking for a broken tile,
A plaque that has become indecipherable,
A piece of slight sculpture attached
To a wall because no one knew where else
To put it. I move through the empty city
And forage for flaking paint on a door,
The dead end, the tiny window, the gate,
The mangy cat, the little yapping dog,
The middle-aged shopper, the half-empty vista.
The shop that sells ordinary electrical goods.

Titian, in his own time of plague, as he worked
On his great Pietà, with his son close by,
Made a little image of them both and placed
It at the bottom right of the painting.
It may be a modest token, a small sign,
To be seen only by those who come
With an eye for such defenceless gifts.
But who can say that in a future when truth
Is back in vogue, this will not stand alone
As something true a man once made?

In his Annunciation, now cleaned up,
Veronese put a glass bowl on a balustrade.
In weak light, it is close to not being there,
Unimportant against the breathless angel
Arrived to surprise the cowering woman.
The bowl breaks the brittle symmetry
Of the architecture and the two figures,
Its pale white smudge, its tear of light,
Unspeaking, unnecessary, begins as whim
And becomes what binds the image to the air.

The study of St Augustine by Carpaccio hangs
In Venice in that room-like gallery, empty now,
The woman at the door almost grateful
There is a visitor. In the painting, I let my eye
Stray from the saint facing the window
As he imagines his own impending death
To a discarded book on the pink floor,
And then to the shadows, all dense, making clear
That as light settles uneasily outside, and water
Licks the stone, what prevails is solid and alone.

CANAL WATER

I am in Venice,
Dreaming of what

It was like
When painters,

Knew which way
To turn

When they had need
For commissions

Or when they sought
Salvation.

There is fog
In the morning

To cloud our
Spirits,

And then sunlight.
In Venice,

Faces in paintings
Are alive with need,

Not just
The main players

But the others
Who stood by

Hardly caring
Who preached sermons,

Who lived
Or who died.

They were busy,
These figures

At the edges,
And did not often think

About redemption,
Much less about

Salvation.
Their faces

Then, and ours now,
Look as though

We are meant, in fact,
For commerce,

Working out margins,
Rates of return.

It is harder,
As the man said,

To imagine
The end of capitalism

Than the end
Of the world.

We hunger, however,
For glare and splash,

An opening
Of the spirit,

The urgent end of
Anything at all.

In the meantime,
I am waiting

For a boat
To take me

To the sanctity
Of the Salute.

The engine
Of the vaporetto

Is grinding
Towards a silence

Like the very first one,
To be broken

Only when

the end
Of capitalism

And the end
Of the world

Appear on the water,
Pursued by the panting

Populace,
The first laden

Down with contracts,
Anti-trust laws,

Overdraft statements,
Old software.

The second
Filled up

With painters
In possession of the new

Colours that
Will be used

To render finality
In all its garishness.

They join forces
Under the domed sky

As the Giudecca
And the Grand Canal

Meet close to
Where I stand

And flow into each
Other, drink

From the waters of the
Exemplary lagoon.

TIEPOLO

The main one, the father,
More than anything,
Loved the pale blue sky.

For his purposes,
It was gentle,
All merciful.

There is no one today
In the side-room
In the church of San Polo

To see the Stations of the Cross
By his son Giovanni Domenico.
In these paintings

Of Our Lord's passion
Leading to his death,
I only want to look

At the sky.
It is my day-off
From peering

At Pilate, at flagellation,
At the crown of thorns.
Young Tiepolo's sky

Is not his father's sky.
It is even paler,
As though the Crucifixion

Took place in early winter
In a tired northern city
Whose scarce light

Throws faint shadow.
His world is windless.
Clouds breeze in

And stay put, as though
Summoned by the painter
Who did not want any more

Turbulence than was
Necessary.
He liked misty light,

Twilight, half-light,
Brushed yellow light.
Just as Jesus

Thought of his Father,
So, too, young Tiepolo
Must have smiled,

At how the skies he made,
Put his father's skies
In the shade.

PRAYER TO ST AGNES

O holy St Agnes, cure me of metaphor!
Make me say exactly what I mean
Without trickery or recourse
To words that are not clear or clean.

O martyr and saint, let life be dull
And make our verses unadorned
And let next year's poems be plainly full
Of signs that lessons have been learned.

The flowers grow, as appointed, from the soil
And do not paint the meadow with delight.
They wither or get picked, which serves to spoil
Our notion, so mistaken on first sight,

That they are sprightly, dancing in the breeze,
Then taking applause, their heads all bowed.
I swear, in all mention of flowers, these
Rich, false words will never be allowed.

In return, please open heaven's gate
So I can see what really is
With no sweet terms to mask my fate
To live in true, unsweetened bliss.

EVE

i.

I say blue when morning begins
And indigo when the night sky
Hardens over us, pinned with stars.

I say moon when its shape appears
In the disappearing light. And I say
Hollow when I look into my hand.

So much taken for granted now
That I am chased by shadows
When once I noticed only

What was solid and complete.
I dream of Adam's voice.
Was that a panting sound or a sigh?

ii.

At first it was head to toe
Until I wanted his breath on mine.
We examined each other,

Like a folded-out map of ourselves,
Fingering, puzzled by
The differences between us.

We tried it this way and that,
I was the impatient one, I have to say.
Strange, we both had a bright idea

At the same time. After that, it seemed
As though we were created to couple
In this sweet new way. It was hard

To do anything else sometimes,
So the trees suffered, burdened
Down with fruit, and the fields,

And some pale animals that emerged
Now and then, and the snakes
Hanging corkscrew from low branches.

iii.

I saw God watching Adam. I saw
The eyes popping out of God's head
At the sight of him

As he fucked with what we later learned
Was wild abandon. I sympathized
With God's jealousy, his pain,

But wished he had not
Displayed such obvious self-pity.
You see, he loved Adam.

Once I watched as
They fondled each other's hair.
From my vantage-point in the tree

I then saw the two of them
Wondering how they might
Do what we had done. I have to say

It was obvious to me.
Odd how they couldn't work it out.
Nothing bothered Adam, but God

Was not pleased, to put it mildly.
I learned that he would have been
Happy to be with either of us. Or

Even with both. He hated being left out.
That was the thing. I liked it
When he licked my neck.

iv.

But, in the end, I bewildered God
More than all creation. We spoke,
But he was never a good listener.

Preferring the sound
Of his own voice
Even when he whispered.

Since he wanted us so much
The decision he made
That we should leave

And that he would be happier
Alone made no sense.
But try telling him that.

v.

I laughed later
When I found out the etymology
Of the word 'paradise'. In all reality,

Paradise was nowhere much; we were
Baked by the sun. Days were long
And there was nothing to do at night.

vi.

Mornings here are lovely, on the other hand,
And the world's words, I never tire of them –
Of Mans First Disobedience, and the Fruit

Would I like to return, you ask,
Just once for a short visit
To re-live old memories?

No, but I would like yesterday to come
Again, wash itself over us,
Fondle us with its shredded beauty.

vii.

In his temper that day, when God told
Us what time would mean, I understood.
I saw the days longing for each other

In a future ready to forget. I alone,
I saw, would register each one,
Like something to be forgiven

And then held up, a bright example,
As we were, when we came into the world,
And lived our disappearing days.

viii.

Adam died two years ago, a night
When the moon was sickle-shaped
And thunder-clouds had cleared.

I was glad of that. I wanted
Adam's fading eyes to see the sky,
Linger on the thought of what we tasted,

A beyond-place that had no end, that might
Have bored others, but we tolerated it
Because what else did we know?

What else do I know now?
I know that God learned to repeat
The word regret *ad infinitum*

Until silence fell. Then he changed.
I wish I could comfort him,
As the world wears out.

ARAFAT IN TUNIS

'As soon as the phone rings, you be ready.
Come downstairs that instant. Don't delay.'
Arranged by the French before they cleared out,
The light over the sea was soft cotton.
Palm trees lined the boulevards, the air
Was sweet; all was quietness, order, ease.

My minders cut the sleepy city open.
The young woman screamed at me to get
Into the car. The driver stood by,
Tense, alert, looking warily around him.
And then we drove at speed, using a route
That made no sense, to the compound.

I took notes, and later I wrote about
What Arafat said. I was the journalist.
But, after all the years, what I recall most
Is the dim light in an ante-room,
And maybe a dozen young men in leather jackets
And tight jeans, his bodyguards,

Sitting or leaning against the wall, studying
Me lazily, eyes hooded, giving nothing away.
I wondered what they did when darkness fell.
Did they eat at a long table, like disciples?
Did they sleep in a row of beds, obedient?
Was one of them a favourite, maybe two?

I liked the poses struck by those men.
In checking each one out, I am sure that
I gazed too much, too unmistakably.
Some glanced back, guarded, then looked away.
And just as I was ushered towards the interview,
A few of them took me in again, unbothered, bored.

JERICHO

i.

The sky at night is full of stars
that outshine
the moon.

Across the narrow gorge
a man with goats
leans against a tree.

My companion pulls at my sleeve
so I will attend
to his warnings.

In an hour or two
the hordes could
take Tel Aviv,

Zip like lightning
over the
Allenby Bridge.

For a while, the washed
light over us is
calm and controlled.

What is the name
of that place,
over to the right?

It is bathed in
blueness, whiteness against
the parched brown.

Like water boiling,
the steam entangling
houses, trees.

Whisper the word oasis:
moisture against
prevailing dryness.

I dream I am old –
teeth missing, knees shaky,
hips painful –

Being helped along
and read to; at night
I barely sleep.

The house is almost dark,
a single room,
a single bed.

The air is like water:
I thrive in its heaviness
without a thought.

My helpers are all around:
the youth who guides me
as I walk,

His mother and aunt
who bring food
and fresh clothes,

His father and cousin
who sit in the doorway
as shops close up.

In the dwindling light,
the birds are
frantic in the air.

Those around me
often look sadly
into the distance.

But that is just the dream.
In the real world, we talk of
danger and strategy.

My companion has no
interest in dusty imaginings
but in territory.

This is Israel. Over there,
the West Bank,
the Hebron Hills.

ii.

Years later, I ask
only to be taken
to the place

I saw from that hill,
shimmering in
the hot light.

I will meet myself
coming towards me,
staying in the shadows.

An old man
in a dry month,
as the poem goes.

I am allowed one
strong, bitter coffee
every day.

I will see a town
under the protection of
The Palestinian Authority.

It is in Area A
as decided by
the Oslo Accords.

There are, of course, ancient
sites; Antony and Cleopatra
were here, and Herod.

Jesus cured
the blind beggars
under the walls.

All around: construction,
but no one is allowed
to dig a well.

The main square is busy
with traffic, like
any other town.

Dreams sliced by the sharp
light become the hard
facts of the here and now.

I go to a barber's shop
and a café, glad to be
indoors from the heat.

We are in a car
waiting to go back
to East Jerusalem.

It does not matter
whether any of us look
behind or not.

VALENTIN'S PRAYER

i.

Who will come into the room
If I play Valentin's Prayer
From Gounod's 'Faust'?

What if some random member
Of the dead came
And joined us here?

Someone lost who
Got wind of the sound
And sought shelter.

It is a starless night
In Cush. I can see
Rosslare Harbour

And a glow in the sky
That must have Wexford town
Below it.

And Tuskar Rock, of course,
That has no choice.
It is programmed to shine.

Since this is a new house,
It is not as though
There are others from before

Who lived in these rooms
And feel that they
Belong here.

ii.

Who will convince me
That someone is not
Breathing now

Against the glass,
Gazing at my reflection
As I move around,

Hearing the prayer
As the singer departs,
Guiding my hand

As I write this,
Staying in my mind
As I turn to face them?

PANGUR

Pangur, a neighbour's cat,
Comes to my flat
For peace and quiet.

He likes to lick
My bare toes
While I type.

But he cannot
Keep himself in check
And soon

He starts to bite.
'Pangur,' I bark,
'If you don't stop,

I will put you back
In the poem written
By that monk.'

BECAUSE THE NIGHT

Not sleeping
And then a night's
Hard sleep.

Waking, unsure
Which room
I am in.

My old friend,
Gone two years,
Was there

Last night
Sitting at a table,
Fully himself.

I know
He is dead.
Even in the dream,

I knew this,
And yet I talked to him,
About ordinary things

Not how he died
Or where he is.
Sometimes,

My mother floats in,
Or my brothers;
Less often

My father, who died
Long before
They did.

And then
The old room in
Hatch Street

Or the top floor
Of Number Two
Harcourt Terrace,

Where I lived
Years ago
Come back,

As though I still
Keep stuff in them
But have stopped

Paying the rent
And must sneak
In and out because

Someone
Is under orders
To waylay me.

Soon I will have
To try and rescue
Books and clothes,

Get back the music
That echoes here
Especially on nights

When you snore,
And I move
Into the study

And sleep in
The day-bed.
And when I wake,

I have no clue
Where I am, what
Bed this is.

But I will get up
And find you,
Alive, real, now,

And the morning starts,
E-mails, the newspaper.
I carry the night

All day, though,
A flight-path,
A way through.

ACKNOWLEDGMENTS

Thanks to the editors of the following journals where these poems, or earlier versions of them, appeared: *Bad Lilies*, *bathmagg*, the *Manchester Review*, *Poetry Ireland Review*, *PN Review*, *the Times Literary Supplement*, *New Poetries VIII*, and the *New York Review of Books*.

I am also grateful to Helene Atwan at Beacon Press and John McAuliffe at Carcanet, and to Catriona Crowe, Hedi El Kholti, Ed Mulhall, and Michael Schmidt.

Colm Tóibín was born in Enniscorthy, Co. Wexford, in 1955. He is the author of ten novels, including *The Master*, *Brooklyn*, and *The Magician*. His work has been shortlisted for the Booker Prize three times and won the Costa Novel Award and the Impac Award. He has also published two collections of stories and many works of nonfiction. He lives in Dublin.